The Larkin Hours

The Larkin Hours

Harry White

Cover design by Shay Culligan
Cover image of the author's grandfather, John White, taken c. 1917 (private collection)
Author photo by courtesy of Patrick Dowling, Rock Photography (Co. Dublin, Ireland)

ISBN: 978-1-63980-633-1

Kelsay Books
502 South 1040 East, A-119
American Fork, Utah 84003
Kelsaybooks.com

For my brother, Frank

Contents

Part One

Part One

Visitors

Does anyone remember 'the visitors'?
The guests shown into the front room,
The *good* room,
With its avian ascent of porcelain geese,
Its untouched monuments
And sullen sofa?
A room in black-and-white,
A family museum, while the going was good.

And so a place for visitors:
Priests often, on their tours of duty,
A doctor, once or twice,
An Australian cousin, loud in the afternoon.

We knew their rightful place, and ours.

My mother broke this code just once,
When 'gypsies' came: two restive, feral boys,
Driven by hunger to our door.
She gently eased them down
Onto the speckled lino of the hall floor
And fed them there and then:
Sandwiches and hot tea from a flask.

They gulped it down and were gone,
Mumbling 'Thank you, Missis,' as they went.
Our curious gaze followed them
Into the darkening firmament.

There was no need to ask
Why the front room had been out of bounds,
Why they huddled and ate at the foot of the stairs.

We knew our rightful place, and theirs.

Tests

Its meaning soured by circumstance,
A harmless cipher for my schoolroom trials
In later life becomes an anxious signature,
A doctor's scrawl: 'I'd like to run some *tests.*'

The word mutates without a moment's notice,
And intimates a void I never knew
Within its youthful comprehensions:
Success or failure now means life or death.

This is the word *tests* in its last extremity:
The schoolroom-word made flesh, diseased or saved,
And longing for a second word, *results,*
Which darkens like a mole, or is reprieved.

Voices

for Méabh Nic Mhaoláin

What I remember best are women's voices.

Mrs McCarthy's shrill squawk,
A cockatoo or goaded parrot
In querulous search of its offspring:
Her wailing screech went down the afternoon.

This now seems cruel.
But I think of a bird-call soured and spoiled
By a thousand hours of strident sorrow.

I loved instead the music of 'Dublin Four,'
The slack, relaxed glissando of my aunt,
Her affluent, drawling vowels
And plosive consonants, her laughter-rills:
A voice pitched in the key of inborn joy.

Voices to me were like compass-points as a boy:
My adorable aunt in the sunny, beckoning south
And Mrs McCarthy cold in her northern howl.
Was either aware of her voice as a permanent soundprint,
A signature, always, everywhere, of warmth or woe?

I just don't know.

The Crush Hall

That afternoon in Rome, the Sistine Chapel
Seemed to be excess, with no relief:
A preposterous glut of frescoes, with porters yelling
'Silence!' in the waiting room of heaven;
The tearful end of time for tourist souls
Lurching through the place in gawping swarms.

I felt as if among the newly-dead,
And strange to this estate, this eery transience.
Pushing towards the light I wanted *out:*
The natural caress of open air,
The chatter and pulse of life outside,
Anything but that awful, frescoed nowhere.

When I emerged at last, it all came back,
Though dormant until then for fifty years:
My first day in assembly, Synge Street school,
Boys swarming and piling into the 'crush hall,'
Teachers yelling and cuffing, with no relief:
'The end of the world,' in short. A vale of grief.

Impressions

for Niall Lynch

Niall Lynch is doing impressions of Nixon
In the ten-minute break, before the Latin starts
And the priest ascends the podium and drones the prayers.

For two minutes, at most, we're with Niall in Washington
Egging him on for 'I was *not* involved,'
And that vigorous headshake. Cries of '*Watergate!*' Jeers.

'Mr President,' one of us says, 'Come clean!'
But Nixon demurs, nods again, and departs,
A defiant, victorious salute as he disappears.

The bell is tolling us back. In better mood,
We bend to our dreary ancients. Their deeds are oblique
In the Latin fog which renders us half-awake . . .

That was fifty years ago, or almost:
My impressions of school, like my Latin, are fading fast,
But Niall's arresting Nixon yet survives. In class,

The priest is maundering; Caesar's Gallic Wars,
Or Ovid in exile, dulled by his parsing prose.
Nixon, in time, will also succumb, I suppose.

An English Lesson

for Conor Galvin

Father Draper had set us a paraphrase of Walter de la Mare's poem, 'The Listeners' as our weekend homework (although no-one was going home). I loved the despair of 'Tell them I came, . . . that I kept my word!' towards the end of the poem, and also the subdued tattoo and menace of 'knocking on the moonlit door' at the beginning. And aware even then, at thirteen, that I was 'good at English,' I re-wrote the poem from the point of view of the ghost-presences who can hear the traveller (the principal personage in the poem) but cannot respond to him. I called my paraphrase 'The Traveller.' I don't remember much else about it, except that it had nothing of de la Mare's metrical length of line or technique, and that it clumped along in the crude iambics of a street ballad ('They listen by night/And they listen by day,' and so on). I 'handed it up' (in the faintly votive formula we used back then for submitting our work) on the following Monday morning, and hoped for the best. There were twenty-six boys in the class, and I knew that Father Draper would identify the three finest paraphrases and read them aloud.

Mine came in second. That seemed a fair-enough result until Father Draper paused before announcing the winner. 'But this, boys,' he said, holding aloft Conor Galvin's exercise copy, 'this is the real thing.' His face was flushed with genuine admiration. Then he began to read Conor's work, which was not a paraphrase, and had nothing whatever to do with 'The Listeners.' Instead, Conor had written an original poem about the contents of his pencil case. And I realised with excruciating immediacy, even before the poem had come to an end, that this was indeed the real thing. Each phrase confirmed this painful verdict, which left me stranded on the shores of second-best. I could sense *at once* the difference between my servile imaginings and Conor's poem.

As far as I can tell, I will take this English lesson to the grave, given that it has preoccupied me now for half a century. I can't recall the details of Conor's poem either, except for its surefooted rebellion against the authority of homework, and the effortless music of its trim and deliberately prosaic disclosures. None of that matters very much, but the trace and stamp of authenticity I heard that Monday morning set me straight. My work listened and complied. His travelled beyond compliance, and entered the domain of art.

A Reunion

for John White

The vast reception hall is suddenly *ours*
In the vacated silence of summer.
Some of us lark and smoke outside,
Self-conscious on the wide, steep ascent
Of the stone-cut steps forbidden to us as boys.
Car-doors are slamming softly in the evening air.

The mood is festive and generous. Sunlight, everywhere,
Slanting across the portico, into the hall,
Softens the marble austerity of the place,
And loosens our exhilarated ease
After an absence of twenty adult years,
And a darkness no-one mentions, not at first.

Those places forbidden to us weren't the worst.
The 'shiny corridor' and the central, carpeted stairs
Were out of bounds: boys discovered in either locale
Would kneel for hours on end in the study hall;
A tiresome penalty, but that was all.
The corridor beneath was something else.

The priests are gallant and generous with the wine.
It quickens the pulse and stride of conversation,
A thickening drift of remembrance, and sheer relief
At being back, and yet being free to go.
We are men of parts, approaching forty,
Immune to the past we shared on the floor downstairs.

Immune but not incurious: one of us dares
'A look for old time's sake,' a brief descent
To the 'dark corridor' and Nineteen Seventy-One.

This feels illicit somehow, or slightly against the grain,
Unwarranted by our present warm repose,
A misadventure better left alone.

The floor of the dark corridor was made of stone,
With metal-edged, narrow staircases at either end.
It ran the length of the school with its base ordeals
And subterranean rites. I don't intend
To number these festering cruelties,
Their foul, sadistic catalogue. Let them sleep.

Except for one: the hounding past all hope,
The unremitting torment, day and night,
Of Christopher Fields. An older boy than us,
Whose hell began the moment he'd opened his mouth
To speak in class two years before,
And someone echoed the awkward burr in his voice.

The malevolent genius of that jeer set loose
A compact, monstrous catch-call.
It followed Fields from dawn to dusk:
The most vicious mockery I have ever known.
Lashed and goaded simply for being there,
He would walk that corridor, his face pressed into the wall.

Poems are shits, sometimes, that is all;
Their mad, unvisited truths repel
The sorry enterprise of writing well.
I spoke to Fields just once or maybe twice
Drawn by the lonely terror of his ordeal,
But was warned away by a priest: 'That boy is untouchable.'

He knew the rules of our tribe were incontrovertible
And rescued me from the merciless taint of compassion,
Which meant that I stood silent and complicit.
For 'Dar-Dar Fields,' the torment went on and on,
His cries and beseechments made his oppressors worse:
They grew more bestial in his tears and pain.

His elderly parents came to the school one day
And took away their broken son.
Even then, as he stumbled towards the car,
Someone softly intoned his catch-call, 'Dar-Dar.'
A final, impromptu reminder of what remained:
That secret, infernal arcadia, obscene and unspent.

Everyone is relieved by our re-ascent
To 1996 and the upper floor:
The past, for now, recedes in the balm of summer,
And plans for dinner blur
The taunt and edge of what went on down there;
Someone outside is knocking on the sunlit door.

Car-doors are slamming softly in the evening air,
Most of us glad to get out of there
And leave the place behind, once and for all.
A priest is smiling and waving on the steps.
He turns to go back before we've reached the gate;
He cannot wait. Soon, he is out of sight.

A Priest's Obituary

His whole life is plotted in Irish placenames
Awkwardly anglicized, and listed one by one:
Where he was born, baptised, and went to school,
A hint of his teenage pieties in the chapel,
His golfing habits, his obedience to the rule,
His summers in Sacramento with that couple
Who eased his anguished forties by their pool,
And rescued his stricken years of doubt.

These travails, of course, are always left out.
What remains is a litany, tame and routinely subdued:
The trail of his country parishes, his date of retirement,
His Golden Jubilee mass, a few terms of endearment
('a wonderful man of the people') he'd slowly acquired,
And the name of the pitiful care home in which he died.
A grainy photograph shows him in Lourdes or Knock,
Absorbed in the care of his grateful flock.

Servile Work

The mid-summer, vernacular boom
Of Sunday mass in the open air
Loudens like an auction.

That blaring voice in my living-room
Ripped from the spine of ancient prayer
Sounds coarse and forceful.

This country-music Christ must sadly be
The one 'who humbled himself to share
In our humanity.'

But let this rest. Let quiet resume.
Grace the day in silence, everywhere.
Disturb no more the tomb.

Postcommunion

for Frank Lawrence

The priest's ablutions towards the end of mass
Were somehow furtive and domestic
In the grand glare of elevation and incense.
He first set the disarray of vessels, lids,
Discarded drapes of white silk to rights,
And stored the newly-dressed ciboria
Within their marble recess
Safely under lock-and-key.
He cadenced as he worked,
With genuflections, whispered prayers,
The soft clink of metal on a dish,
A restive congregation at his back.

Everything was in the mode of aftermath,
Faintly plaintive, and hurried:
A swift splash of water and wine to purify his fingers,
Poured by the acolyte,
Who hovered with his cruets near the priest,
Like a waiter serving at table.
The priest meanwhile was swirling and sifting,
Drinking off the residue, inclining the chalice for more.
A second, deeper draught would follow,
And then the scouring-out of the chalice's innermost meaning,
With a linen cloth twisted and crumpled
In the soaking-up of evidence.

At last the chalice was re-dressed,
The burse and sumptuous veil
Like a miniature hat and coat
Covering everything up for decency's sake
As if nothing at all had happened.
Soon he would bear it away,
His left hand gripping the chalice stem within,
His right hand flat and firm upon the burse,
The crumpled linen beneath, a stained chemise
Hidden from public view:
Lovers departing their private sanctuary
And drifting among their secrets and the crowds outside.

Rites of Departure

A small ceremony of farewell on my last afternoon:
Between packing and leaving, Kent would ask, 'All set?'
A question with only one answer. I'd glance at my phone,
And then at the house and gardens, and always the deck,
As if to absorb them completely, until I got back.
Then a drive to the airport, with Kent's 'All set?' still in motion:
'Arrivals.' 'Departures.' Embraces. On my way.
A recessional tread to the gate on my very last day.
Except *not* my last day, or my last mid-Atlantic night,
Or even my last dread of turbulence in mid-flight.
But what if it were? I'd scarcely be *all set* then:
But terrified, groping for words, and hurtling down . . .

*****

My father was groping his way from bed when it happened:
His flight ran into trouble, with no way out.
He simply said *I'm going,* and that was that.
When I saw him next, his body was waxed and waked,
All set for his departure and descent.
I touched and kissed him, though he was long since gone,
As if I'd reached the airport much too late
Or hopelessly tried to recall him from the gate.
I thought of his flight path, with no return or end
Except for his certain decay in the cold ground . . .

*****

I’ve been on board for hours, and light is breaking
Over the Irish coast. People are waking.
The cabin stirs with something like relief,
At least to me. These are the rites I love:
The shutters up, the safely-stowed assurances
Of swift deliverance, journey’s end. The plane
Descends, descends, descends, pushing through cloud
And juddering, turbulent gusts. We’re almost there.
The readying jolt and strut of landing gear,
The cabin flooded with shafts of sun, the tranquil
Glide and pull to sudden earth, then touchdown,
Like the grace of his swift departure: *Going,* then gone.

Neighbouring Sounds

for Reda and Marius Ginaitai

Marius is trying to start his car next door.
I can hear the engine's aging, iron shudder
And rasping piston-cough,
Until, at last, it connects and begins to turn over,
The cylinders clearing, like lungs inhaling air.

I suddenly think of my grandfather Jack,
Younger than I am now, and for years before,
Hacking and coughing for breath,
Starting each fitful day with this chronic attack
Which my father recalled as 'a pitiful thing to hear.'

I wish I'd known him. Gassed in the First World War,
He remained a private man for the rest of his life
And died before I was born.
He was photographed in Cologne, near a courtyard bar,
His uniform gleaming and spruce, like a brand-new car.

Ironing and Airing

The space between my mother and her neighbour
Seated on a wall in early summer
Is whatever they are saying.

It occupies the centre of this photo
With its sensual affordances of light
Framed by sheds and garden trees.

Between the sheds, both women are in profile,
Oblivious of the camera's graceful gaze,
Intent instead upon each other.

My mother is sleeveless and aproned. A washing line
Depends and sways in the evening's gathering breeze.
Let nothing impugn these intimacies.

Accounts

My mother said that she was ‘from the gypsies;’
My father said he’d once been a circus clown:
We thought for years that these accounts were spurious,
But later we saw that neither one was wrong.

Sleeping Quarters

First

Snug and cocooned in my lair above the ocean,
We're diverted to Singapore.
The women are coiffed and seductive-smart;
They bring champagne to my sequestered door.
I am the object of their groomed perfection:
Who could possibly ask for more?

Business

Glancing beyond the confines of this pleasure-dome,
I become differently aware
Of business class and its sepulchral gloom.
The cabin is like an elongated hospital room,
With people sleeping everywhere:
A ward of bodies reclining in mid-air.

Economy

In the cramped conditions of the floor below
Sleep is fitful and fugitive. Although
This fourteen-hour confinement will not pass
Without a thousand different bodily contortions
In its quest, just a lucky few will find it:
But for most, it's intermittent or suspended.

Emergency

‘Let him sleep,’ I heard the cardiologist say
After I’d spent the night in an upright chair
In the corridor of a hospital ward near here:
We were the passenger-patients in a fretful queue,
Attended by nurses like cabin crew,
Who remained on board after we went on our way.

The Larkin Hours

Waking at four to Larkin's 'soundless dark'
I'd half-recall illicit dreams of her
Or start from anxious sleep:
Those innocent hours are gone.

Larkin feared the void, but he was wrong
To dread that 'sure extinction.' I would keep
My hope of *nothing, nowhere*
As a merciful end, not stark.

Instead, my feeble vision is an afterlife
Akin to here, or something very close—
The long, unhappy queue
Of Larkin's 'wrong beginnings:'

The harsh ordeals, the losses and the winnings
All as they were before, but somehow new,
Indecent and obtuse:
A pointless second strife.

Or worse—the bullying heat of endless bliss,
The preposterous Hosanna without end:
A beatific boredom,
The infantile carousel.

So give my regards to Heaven and to Hell,
I've seen enough of both. I want the freedom
To depart and then descend
Into the sleep of nothingness.

But God won't grant me that, and therein lies
My fearful vigil in the Larkin hours.
Instead, He's just begun:
His world is yet to come.

'World without end:' that formula, for some,
Endures with obstinate grace, whereas I shun
This hope that overpowers
My natural demise.

Colours

for Brendan Doherty

Brendan D. is here to paint two rooms,
The walls stripped bare in readiness, the contents shrouded.
Prepped in surgical white, the furniture seems
Remote and sombre-still beneath the sheets,
Like statues veiled in church, or bodies crowded
Within a makeshift morgue. Each room secretes
Its ordinary meaning under these chastening folds
Of motionless cloth. Something lapses and yields.

Brendan is swift and skilled; he dips and brushes
With smooth strokes across the passive walls:
They brighten evenly under his hand and eye.
Yesterday's stained and jaundice-yellow stretches
Steadily disappear. The whole room fills
With lustrous colour, and quickens into life.
He leaves it to air and dry; takes a break;
Appraises the room next door; resumes his work.

When he's done, the rooms will soon recover
Their wonted estate, freshly revealed and restored
In gleaming greens and whites. Their spectral pallor
Will fall away, like a hospital gown exchanged
In a spurt of deep relief for life on the streets.
Furniture, paintings and books will be set to rights.
I know my future is hospital-grey or black,
But for now, I'm free of those colours: take a look.

The Gardens of Harmonious Interest

for Xiao Mei White

Something is perturbed in this translation:
Harmonious interest cannot signify
Your placid gardens in the rain.
This English falters in its stilted pomp.

The Chinese must be otherwise, and closer
To the graces that recur in spring,
The sunlit majesty of everything
In the wake of winter's sullen sleep.

This majesty is yours, from blade to blade
Of grass, from every hedgerow, plant and bloom
You've bedded, pruned or weeded,
From every living thing you've shaped or seeded.

But the gardens are excessive as I write,
With surplus growth. The foliage of summer
Has supervened the boundaries of their syntax,
Like someone who has far too much to say.

The laurel hedges, getting in the way,
Are straggling towards the sky:
They spoil this *hortus clausus* I adore
And besiege its trim composure.

Before the winter comes you will restore
The privacy and shape of this enclosure:
A tractor-mounted cutter will subdue
And curb its elemental anarchy.

The meaning of this seasonal redress
Is a horticultural grammar that precedes
And underwrites the very enterprise
Of *gardening,* harmonious or otherwise.

A grammar that exactly intervenes
Between the wilderness of natural growth
And every floral grace you've wrought
Is not instinctive: it has to be acquired.

You've had to learn its structures and devices
Like a language that is nurtured and inspired
By the intercourse of universal laws
With the individual heft of lived experience.

The lived experience of those trees you planted
On the fifth day of May, ten years ago,
Exemplifies this intimacy between
Your science then, and what those trees now mean.

Those fragile saplings that you bedded down
Are now deep-rooted, tall and fully-grown.
Their signatures of grace depend each spring:
A canopy of white blossoms, blessing everything.

Gardens overgrow, and households yield
Beneath the fell of accidental time,
When entropy prevails, and all is lost
To a wailing ambulance and the withered past.

Against that sure decline, your tranquil gardens
Germinate and grow into a refuge
Of *harmonious interest* after all:
The phrase itself is unperturbed, at last.

It settles with impassive, Asian calm
And assuages these misgivings. For the rest,
I hope and marvel. Only you, my dear,
Can cultivate this harmony, year on year.

Tides

for Fiachra White

Before the tide ebbs
he is shin-deep,
knee-deep,
hip-deep,
in the warmth and bodily sway
of salt water.

Later,
the ridges of sand
will dismay
the soles of his feet,
the tidal wash and caress
will drift away.

He is sempiternal
on the beach,
or thinks he is,
or feels he is:
a nearly-naked, stock-still boy,
beyond my reach.

Games

for Dara White

Games for you, and churches for me:
Both of us somehow staring hard at screens.
Mine are filled with light and startled saints,
Yours with silent armies and labyrinths.

What can we hope to find there, other than refuge
From the world as it was, and is, and ever shall be?
Never an easy place for you or me.

So let these consolations multiply:
My naves and aisles, your quests and interfaces,
Blissful, populous, solitary; making sense
Of prayer and player, each in his own enterprise.

I may never come upon you in the apse
Of a silent church, nor you upon me online;
But we are father and son, in your game or mine.

Name-Dropping

Years ago, a hostess, brash and loud,
Was brandishing famous names among the silver
And braying about her doubtful claims to intimacy.
We in the dying light, with lowered heads,
Were trying not to laugh.

She sailed on without a blush, unbowed,
Sexy even, glittering in tall tales
Before her silent guests. Our dumb complicity
Deepened with every preposterous name she dropped;
No-one said a word.

Decades later, I am dropping names,
But not as she did, over the waning light:
Instead, it is my effort to retrieve
That lowers heads, or when alone at night,
Makes me feel absurd.

The Well

Nothing seems to stir today.

All I can hear is the lowered bucket
Swaying against the deep of the concrete well.
The rope won't tighten: it comes up slack
And almost weightless.

Yesterday's hoist of pool-dark, gleaming water
Is mocked by this pitiful yield,
Like a manly stream of urine in sunny youth,
And the spatter of piss that comes with getting old.

I crane my neck into the useless void
Of dank and dark descent,
Straining to see what isn't there.

Straightening up to these arch and stilted likenings,
This vacuous shorthand for despair,
I curse my dull complaints and walk away.

For now, there's nothing more to say.

The Emperor in the Armchair

Everyone has encountered him:
Some widowed tyrant in an armchair,
Delivering sour speeches
From the throne of discontent.

In this particular instance, I recall
A wheelchair and a massive wife—
His stupendous entourage, his double-act,
Their girth impending in the hall.

She was his straight-man, faithfully translating
All his bickering bile of blacks and queers
Into the quiet asides of in-law bliss
And the stage-business of drinks and easy chairs.

So yes, I saw through all this, without pity
For his plump paws upon that loathsome belly
Or his useless legs or wheezy gasps for air:
In case you've missed it, I didn't care.

He was the emperor in the iron armchair,
The bringer of hatred and domestic woe,
The schoolyard braggart, still on the go,
And she was his accomplice and his empress.

Now they lie together under the gravel
And sin-whitening pebble stones near the sea,
With only a coastal breeze to catch their babble,
Remembered otherwise by no-one, except me.

Seeing Someone

Waiting for someone else that afternoon,
He saw her walking towards him through the snow.

He knew, against all odds, it must be her:
His hammering heart told him so.

As she came nearer, he swayed on the edge of collapse
And slumped down hard on a seat made of stone.

The impact restored him and lessened his racing pulse.
He began to feel better—lightheaded at most.

He stood up to embrace her, and suddenly saw he was wrong:
Her sylph-like perfection had vanished and gone.

The beautiful woman he'd taken for her met his stare,
And briefly smiled as she passed him and went on elsewhere.

The afternoon relapsed; the dying sun
And disappointed snow eclipsed by rain.

He stood there; stranded by his loss anew
When the person he'd been expecting came into view.

A Dream-Vision

It did not seem at all surreal in sleep
To find she'd gone.
The whiteness of her voided sheets,
Her gleaming boots erect against the wardrobe,
A boarding pass, a Roman handbag, make-up:
The whole room blanched with absence.
The mild commotion downstairs in Reception
Confirmed the haste in which she had departed.

He raced through open fields and narrow gardens
And felt his gaze drawn upwards, towards the sky.
He saw the motion of her deepening wing-strokes
Which brought dismay, but no surprise.
A swan in natural flight:
He knew it to be her as she climbed clear,
And knew as well what this dream-vision meant.

He saw her next incapable of speech,
Caged and sorrowful, aching to be free.
He read the meaning of her tears:
You have to let go of me.
He thought of how her body arched
And shuddered in the snow at their first kiss.
But nothing now remained of this,
Except for his beseechment and her frown.

And then he woke, and wrote the whole thing down.

Primary Source

> The supplementary parts are beautifully composed, and the clarinet entry in the Gloria, bars 8–12, is obviously the work of a master. At that time, however, Haydn's authorship could not be regarded as certain, because the original parts in Eisenstadt were lost. As it turns out, these parts were hastily stuffed into a chimney . . . when the Russian troops occupied the castle in 1945; they were later rediscovered, undamaged, and this writer has since examined them.
>
> —H.C. Robbins Landon, in the preface to his 1961 edition of Joseph Haydn's *Missa in Tempore Belli* ['Mass in Time of War'] (1796)

Adumbrations of the clarinet, *chalumeau*-soft in Eisenstadt,
Lost and then recovered, when the soldiers had departed.
Warming up the texture, although unauthenticated,
Hidden in a chimney-piece: the rough pillage thwarted.

On my desk, the miniature score, with the clarinet parts restored;
Robbins Landon has vetted them, their authorship now secured.
These 'supplementary parts' are primary in more than one sense:
Bars eight and nine in the Gloria are a fleeting Jazz incipience.

Why should these graces matter, in the mortal tumult of war,
With the timpani menacing the *Agnus Dei,* and Napoleon at the door?
They're scarcely more than an afterthought, heard above the fray,
Irrepressibly added by Haydn at the end of a difficult day.

Obviously the work of a master, this sudden riff in the blue,
This sun-shaft caressing the feverish louds and softs below
Is a beautiful face in the crowd, the relief of a woman's laughter
That vanishes into the soundscape of music in time of war.

The mass itself survives, though Europe should collapse
And the volume is turned up louder on this sad eclipse.
Let the soldiers come again, for all I care:
You, my love, are my primary source. That much is clear.

Three Commonplaces

'At First'

Some law of disillusion preponderates
In the aftermath of 'At first,'
It almost always signals a turn for the worse.

'At first' undermines a rapturous beginning,
Or consigns it irretrievably to the past:
Nothing so lovely can last.

'Day Five'

McArthur is losing hope, I find:
It is Day Five, and the pressure is starting to tell.
He says he is thoroughly frightened, and feels unwell.

Last night, I saw his face in a pistol-flare
Sent up by the Hun. He looked like one of the damned:
I foolishly thought of El Greco in No Man's Land.

'At Last'

There is no general treachery in 'At last.'
It swiftly remediates distress
In its adverbial gloss.

It lets the reader know Day Five has passed,
And signifies that everyone is safe:
'At last' sighs with relief.

Winter Song

(after Schubert's setting of Der Leiermann, by Wilhelm Müller)

for Lorraine Byrne Bodley

The song is winter-dead and barely breathing.
The piano circles around a sombre drone
And echoing dirge, before a note is sung.
What is the sound the singer makes? A wail?
A soft lament? He's in a trance of grief.

He sleepwalks through the verse, until
He comes upon its end. At first, he sees
An aged, finger-numbed and barefoot man
Standing on the ice, beyond the village,
Cranking out a tune that no-one wants.

A beggar with his ever-empty bowl,
Growling dogs surrounding him on the street
As people hurry past without a glance,
Anxious not to meet his eye, or hear
The fractured music from his chordophone.

At last, the two men are alone,
Facing each other across the darkening street,
Complicit in each other's knowing solitude.
Music takes the reins of German verse
And lifts the voice to press its meaning home.

'Oh, strange old man,' the singer cries, 'shall I
Now go with you? And will you turn your lyre
To my songs?' The piano's sure reply
Is the tender but implacably mortal sound
Of journey's end.

A Watercolour by Jean Hale

for Jose Matera, and in memory of Kent Gillespie

-1-

Her brushstrokes are my silent Canada,
Tremendous in the August afternoon.
The air is undisturbed and sultry-still
Upon the cusp and drifting tide of sleep:
She has painted summer heat.

High trees are darkening in a river;
Water floods the foreground like a mirror
That dissolves the scene of which it dreams:
A teeming camouflage of reds and greens
Surrendering to its own reflection.

Sequestered, and peripheral to this view,
Two people, sitting on a riverbank,
Diminutive beneath the trees and sky,
Are scarcely seen at first.
But afterwards, they haunt my inward eye.

Their posture intimates unease:
Legs drawn up, they're staring at the ground
In silent solitude, and yet together.
They seem oblivious to the drowsy weather;
Perhaps they just have nothing much to say.

And do they walk contentedly away,
Out of the frame of my imagined grief,
Persisting now for twenty years?
Perhaps they had no cause for tears,
And whatever I had seen just wasn't there.

But nor is this a blameless afternoon:
Although the artist might be unaware
Or careless of her visionary impulse
To compromise the innocence of summer,
Her landscape is unsettled in my view.

These people are not incidental to
Her general subject-matter or intent;
Their presence undermines the summer scene
And unravels its composure:
I cannot supervene this tense disquiet.

Or is it that my overreaching eye
Cannot now unsee or unimagine
Its own interpretation
In the colder light of common sense?
Is art distorted by experience?

Give me back the seasonal caress
I felt when I first saw this painting
In the perfect summer stillness of your house.
Give me back that signature
Of sacramental bliss that's gone forever.

-2-

Paintings do not age, but when I asked
To see this one again while writing here,
You sent a photo of it through your phone
And I spotted something new
That neither one of us could see at first:

Within the doubtful Eden I'd remembered
(That bowed, disquieting couple, and the landscape)
The camera flash has captured your reflection,
Partial and submerged among the grey
And green pastels already there.

It is visible through the murky flow of water
In which your shoulder, forearm, slender wrist
And shapely fingers now appear
As if they had been painted in by her,
Then it vanishes where the trees and water meet.

And that's not all. This photograph has now
Usurped the painting which it represents,
Augmented it, somehow, by these inclusions.
Your bodily grace belongs to it forever:
It renders the original incomplete.

After we'd discovered your reflection,
Your husband's face appeared among the trees.
And nor can this be unimagined by
My Rorschach eye: he gazes down
Upon the river, and on you.

It’s not as if you haven’t seen him too:
The artist’s brushstrokes, goaded by our need,
Resolve themselves into this looming visage
To complete the picture’s meaning
Now decisively removed from summer’s grasp.
There isn’t any further need to ask
About Jean Hale’s original intentions,

Which cannot be redeemed in any case
Against the presence of your husband’s face
And your bodily reflection in the river.

Somewhere in a studio, near your home,
She is painting summer heat.
She daubs the trees and sky, the darkening flow,
And adds that brooding couple on the grass.
Thirty years or more since then have passed.

And now your comprehending photograph,
A gloss upon her work that amplifies
Whatever she had meant, is in her way.
Or in the way of art; although
That’s not quite what I’d hoped to say.

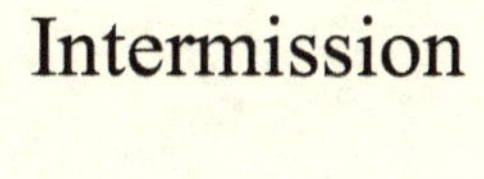

Intermission

My Doubtful Precepts

Art

- Art invalidates experience. Those who file past the painting or close the novel are often impoverished in the aftermath of turning back to their own lives.
- Beckett's writings are a vital expression of Protestantism, specifically in relation to Joyce's Catholic extravagance.
- Beethoven's violence is of the same ferocity as a street-corner assault.
- The Spanish guitar is improbable.
- T.S. Eliot exchanged art for the consolations of religion.
- Yeats's authority is equestrian.
- The right to silence is the enemy of popular culture.
- Loud music is also the truest signature of the abyss.
- It is a commonplace that Vivaldi's sound-world extends to and prefigures the factory floor and the production line. But it also inhabits the stupendous majesty of the hotel lobby with its muted aquatic tumult, swaying ferns and glassy marble. There, it soothes innumerable assignations, business meetings and stray backpackers, who have wandered into a room in the emperor's palace.
- A partial theory of church music: without dissonance, consonance would have nothing to redeem.

Youth

- To have escaped the merciless governances of the schoolyard is an incremental and lifelong relief.
- Without the dizzying proximity of a sensual aunt, male adolescence is strikingly deprived.
- A sinister uncle is often the first shark in the harbour.
- Old age reproves youth with laughable serenity.
- 'Boxing Day:' in my Irish Catholic childhood, this phrase was the first tremor of Protestantism.
- Not all children are adversaries.

Sex

- Obedience is lust. Shorn of its original meaning (devout adherence to a higher cause), the word has re-entered the lexicon as a synonym for erotic enslavement and bliss.
- Beauty voids the questionnaire.
- The truest regions of desire are both commonplace and inadmissible.
- 'Men' and 'Women' may be receding as exclusive categories of interest, but tallness and sexual lustre continue to hold hands.
- Short men in the company of tall women: within the precious sphere of vanity, only one thing is more disdainful.
- Crude fingers drain desire.
- A handsome feminist wearing high boots has her feet firmly on the ground.
- Physical beauty, like intelligence, is magnificently unfair.
- We live in the unmistakable age of androgyny.

Language

- The subjunctive mood unsettles consent.
- The past tense is the refuge of post-truth.
- It is supererogatory to resort to Latin for a nobler style.
- 'All I ask,' no matter how modest the request, is a formula doomed to refusal.
- Grammar relies on a slovenly but efficient bus driver.
- 'Eurocentric' and 'Eccentric' are now almost indistinguishably pejorative qualifiers.
- The ampersand is a belittlement. Who can fail to mistake its cheeky, music-hall advertences, its billboard bravado? The names in its vulgar clutch are subtly abashed.

Customs and Usages

- Surnames are now a reluctance.
- Opening and closing salutations have become occasions of resentment, shyness, or impatient contempt.
- Chivalric names ('Godfrey,' 'Rupert') in a secular age diminish the bearer: a semi-detached house cannot be castellated without ridicule.
- Overfamiliarity is a concept alien and even offensive to the current age, but it turns the heart cold nevertheless.
- Waiting at table should not comprehend an account of the server's part-time degree in urban geography.
- Equality, Diversity and Inclusivity are significantly public virtues. Thus far, however, moral commandments have been perennially assailed by the private impulse to sin against them.
- A true history of personal pronouns in the present day: the dissolution of gender and of the possessive case.

Friends and Enemies

- Intimacy fosters dismay.
- My worst enemy remains silent.
- Betrayal is the recreation of psychopaths.
- Life is a succession of sad partings.
- Old money unseats and recalls even the kindest heart.
- The truly unforgivable is very rare, and it admits of no remission other than hypocrisy.
- To show contempt for the work of a friend is usually a fatal inadvertence.

Miscellaneous

- Fear is the indispensable condition of morality.
- Sadness often beggars explanation.
- Rome has entered upon its second decline and fall.
- Domestic tyranny is an incessant and mortal siege.
- Dreamless sleep is the elusive longing of old age.
- A coarse priest saying mass through a loudhailer is an absurd horror worthy of Bosch.
- *L'école, c'est moi.*

Part Two

Unsayable Lights

in memory of SJH

I

Words deepening, entering 'the sense of touch:'
This, from first to last, his visible signature,
The wherefore of his hair-fine, perfect pitch
And subterranean ear. He'd listen for
What no-one else could hear: the deepest ligature
Binding sound and sense, and irrigate
The topsoil of dried-out language in its cause,
With words like 'vetch' and 'sluice.'
Mined and newly-purposed, bedded-down,
His lexicon was from a souterrain
And undergrowth of soundings long inert,
Pulsing steadily through his antennary art
And tendrilled syntax. Whereupon he found
Just intonation in the opened ground.

II

‘The song of a tubular steel gate in the dark:’
He lets you hear its sigh and softened screech,
An iambic drag of steel across the concrete.
The bolt is then shot home and does its work,
Curbing, cadencing the lustral wash of the verse
With a firm, full close. This sets a space
Between his rich retrievals and the heft
Of what he has to say. The line will tighten
In the sestet, its deliverance nearer,
But still beneath the surface of the poem,
Until its metamorphic surge of pressure
Overcomes the lexical delta-wave
Of ordinary usage. In its place,
His rueful alchemy. Valedictory grace.

III

Shires dreaming wine: even there,
In this surreal image from Glanmore,
A Saxon noun that dreams beyond its ken
Intimates new vistas. A European
Amplitude of poetry lies within
His vowel-shifts and sentient invocations:
Homer, Virgil, Dante, Milosz, Herbert
Illuminate the coastline of his verse,
Like urban constellations seen below
The cloudless skies from a plane at night.
They offer reassurances of light
Against the dark immensements that engulf
The reader's sight, through which his work acquires
A *clearance,* like the sun streaming through shires.

IV

After he came south his verse grew warmer,
A 'purple-stained mouth' beyond the frost-line
Of bog earth and the wintering-out of sterner
Landscapes from his dark agrarian fugues.
All this softened into colour-wash
And wavering heat. A lingering over moods
And sultry cadences, a blurred montage
Gradated slowly like a focus-pull
To hover on the precipice of meaning.
But sometimes in the lush of summer dreaming,
On the lakeshore of an Arcadian afternoon,
Bad news from Ireland surfaced all too soon,
Drenching and sluicing like an iron dredger
That rifted the poem, and brought back colder weather.

V

His *in memoriam* verse ('so much, too much')
Was sometimes an ablative absolute of remembrance
(*These words having been said . . .*), like a scriptural sentence
Or a psalmist's plangent outcry. He might touch
Upon the awful void and harrowing circumstance
Of sudden death—an accident, or worse—
But his diction was mostly reticent, other-purposed,
And likely to catch you off-guard. He'd advance
Straight past the signatures of grief,
And take a lesser road into the deep
Of someone's mid-life radiance, finding there
A quietude that draws the poem together.
After which, a swift departure, always:
The psalmist's *And my tongue shall announce thy praise.*

VI

What is your ‘apology for poetry’?
And what is mine for music, in a country
That is comfortless and deaf, unless
The lyre is tuned to language? No-one scruples
Over poetry as the highest art
And noblest jurisdiction of the tongue:
When Irish verse sails towards Byzantium
Its hedge schools and its singing schools are one.
But music is a secondary art
Wherever ‘words alone are certain good,’
Or at most an aspiration. Would
We have it otherwise, a force apart?
While fruit decays and dies upon the briar
I listen for assuagements from your lyre.

VII

Industrial slats of dark ocean green
Mildly caress my face as I push through
To gain admittance to this shopping mall,
This unforbidden city known as *Friendship*
Or *Large World:* a vast, six-storied hall
On the edge of Dalian in Northeast China.
There isn't a mote of natural light. Its aura
Is subdued, penumbral, easeful, pensive;
It could be night. People drift and disperse
Into the web and maze of stalls and shops
While I stand stock-still, listening to the *omphalos*
Of Buddhist chanting from the lowermost floor.
A store-keeper catches my eye, then smiles and nods
In silent comprehension of my awe.

VIII

Field notes from the tremor underground
Of ghosted escalators, urban corners
Where I gazed into the void of his departures:
A coldness after body-heat, his hand
Released from mine; the kindness of his back,
His signature-grin, before the city traffic
Absorbed his watchful interest. I would stare,
And wish us yet together, anywhere.
And then my own, invariable uphill trek
Into the baggage-handler's endless dream
Of transit. There I'd join the thickening stream
And surge of homeward travellers to connect
My loss to theirs in harmless small-talk. Some,
Mostly women, saw how much I missed him.

IX

My two sons, one of whom now lives near there,
Led me one December to Windermere.
To reach the water's edge from the thronged town,
A frozen slope of mud. As we went down
In single file, I felt their guiding warmth,
Secure at sixty, safe between them both.
Beside the churning lake, beneath the fells,
My glad recital of 'The Daffodils'
While they were skimming stones across the waves,
Together with my grandson. Now I think
Of Devenish with Fiachra, years before,
And of the pilgrimage we both made there
To read your poem aloud under the tower
And 'carved, monastic heads,' above the water.

X

I thought his poems had lost a lot of weight:
Some of them spare and flat-packed, prepped and scrubbed.
'Quickened,' he'd have said, and stripped of ornament,
The verses leaner, shorter, and much less ambient.
Even the long-limbed poems, although luxuriant
And steeped in wondrous music, countenance death.
Deep shafts of light in the furrowed ground:
Bands of mist over a dream with no sound.
The sense of *Four Last Songs,* of letting go
Is gently unrelieved; a farewell tour
Of 'midnight and closedown' on the radio.
A kite ascending the heavenly blue vanishes
Into (and in) the very last song:
A deft perfection of utterance, and then he's gone.

Acknowledgments

The title poem in this collection responds to Philip Larkin's poem, 'Aubade,' which was first published in 1977.

The phrase *hortus clausus* in 'The Gardens of Harmonious Interest' literally means a 'closed garden,' i.e., one that is completely enclosed by walls or hedges.

The 'intermission' between Parts One and Two is a mere caprice: I am grateful to several readers who encouraged me to include it nevertheless.

'Unsayable Lights' responds to Seamus Heaney's 'Glanmore Sonnets' from *Field Work,* published in 1979; the sequence also glosses lines from 'At the Water's Edge' from the same collection (IX), 'District and Circle' (VIII), and 'Quitting Time' (II) from *District and Circle,* published in 2006 and 'A Kite for Aibhín' (X) from *Human Chain,* published in 2010.

Many people read several of these poems in draft: in particular, I would like to thank Anika Babel, Lorraine Byrne Bodley, Marc Caball, Eoghan Corrigan, Karina Daly, Nicole Grimes, Frank Lawrence, Josephine Matera, Hannah Millington, Eva-Maria de Oliveira Pinto and Frank White for their entirely constructive care of my work throughout.

www.ingramcontent.com/pod-product-compliance
Lightning Source LLC
LaVergne TN
LVHW050942080826
845145LV00004B/1369

* 9 7 8 1 6 3 9 8 0 6 3 3 1 *